CONSTANTINE CAVARNOS' WORKS SURVEYED

VOLUME II

OTHER BOOKS BY
JOHN E. REXINE

SOLON AND HIS POLITICAL THEORY

RELIGION IN PLATO AND CICERO

AN OUTLINE OF TACITUS

AN OUTLINE OF THUCYDIDES

THE HELLENIC SPIRIT:
BYZANTINE AND POST-BYZANTINE

AN EXPLORER OF REALMS OF ART,
LIFE, AND THOUGHT
(CONSTANTINE CAVARNOS'
WORKS SURVEYED, VOLUME I)

CONSTANTINE CAVARNOS

CONSTANTINE CAVARNOS' WORKS SURVEYED

VOLUME II

A CONTINUATION OF THE VOLUME
*AN EXPLORER OF REALMS OF ART,
LIFE, AND THOUGHT*

By

JOHN E. REXINE, Ph.D., Litt.D.

INSTITUTE FOR BYZANTINE
AND MODERN GREEK STUDIES
115 Gilbert Road
Belmont, Massachusetts 02178
U.S.A.

Typesetting:
E. Marshall Publishing & Translation Services
Brookline, Massachusetts

First edition, 1997

Copyright 1997 and published by THE INSTITUTE FOR
BYZANTINE AND MODERN GREEK STUDIES, INC.
115 Gilbert Road, Belmont, Massachusetts 02178-2200, U.S.A.

Printed in the United States of America

Library of Congress Catalog Card Number: 97-61106

Clothbound ISBN 1-884729-27-4
Paperbound ISBN 1-884729-28-2

PREFACE

Soon after the appearance of the first volume of the present work, entitled *An Explorer of Realms of Art, Life, and Thought: A Survey of the Works of Philosopher and Theologian Constantine Cavarnos*, the author, Professor John E. Rexine, began writing reviews on Cavarnos' books that were published following its appearance in 1985. He planned to publish a second volume of reviews, pertaining to the works of Cavarnos published after that year. Judging from the latter's prolific productivity as a writer in the past, he believed that around the year 2000 he would have written enough reviews of new books authored by Cavarnos to constitute a new volume comparable in size to the first.

Unfortunately, Rexine's progressively deteriorating health resulted in his untimely death, in October of 1993. By that time he had written twenty-one reviews of books authored by Cavarnos and published after 1985. All of these reviews but one have been published in periodicals. The unpublished one is a review of *New Library, Volume Two*. Regarding this book, Rexine wrote to Cavarnos on September 24, 1992: "I wish to thank you for sending me volume II of your *New Library*.

I have skimmed it and know that I'll enjoy reading it." On July 12, 1993—three months before his death—Rexine wrote to him: "*St. Vladimir's Theological Review* has my review of your *New Library II*." For some unknown reason, that journal has not published this review.

The twenty published reviews have been gathered together in the present volume. The unpublished one has not been included, because we do not have the typescript.

These reviews are written in a laconic style—reflecting Rexine's Spartan heritage—clear, lively, and to the point. They constitute an extremely valuable aid to understanding and appreciating Cavarnos quite extensive work, which now numbers over sixty books.

The general layout of this volume follows that of the preceding one. The reviews have been grouped under two main headings: "Philosophical Works" and "Theological Works"—seven under the first heading and thirteen under the second. For the sake of brevity and explicitness, the title of this book has been reduced from the nine words of the first volume to four, taken from the subtitle of that volume. For convenient reference, we have added an Index of Proper Names and an Index of Subjects.

THE PUBLISHERS

ACKNOWLEDGMENTS

Acknowledgment is made of assistance from the Colgate Research Council and the Colgate Humanities Division Faculty Development Fund in the preparation of this book. The author also wishes his readers to note that occasionally omissions have been made in reprinting the reviews in order to avoid unnecessary repetition; that many corrections and revisions have been made throughout the book; that the chapter headings of the book are *the titles* of Dr. Cavarnos' works; and that twenty books are discussed in as many chapters.

The author wishes to thank the editors of *Diakonia, The Orthodox Theological Review, The Greek World, The Hellenic Chronicle, The Patristic and Byzantine Review,* and *St. Vladimir's Theological Quarterly* for publishing the original versions of his reviews and for the permission to include them in this volume, and Dr. Cavarnos for permission to use the title pages and many illustrations from his books.

CONTENTS

PART I
PHILOSOPHICAL WORKS

PART II
THEOLOGICAL WORKS

CONSTANTINE CAVARNOS

BIOGRAPHICAL NOTE ON
JOHN E. REXINE*

Dr. John E. Rexine, who was Charles A. Dana Professor of the Classics and Chairman of the Classics Department of Colgate University at Hamilton, N.Y., died on October 23, 1993, at Hamilton. The son of Efstratios and Athena (Glekas) Rexine, natives of Sparta, he was born in Boston, Massachusetts, on June 6, 1929. He was married to Elaine (Lavrakas) on June 16, 1957, of whom he had two sons: John E., Jr., and Michael Constantine, and one daughter, Athena Elisabeth Hodge.

A graduate of Harvard College in 1951, John received his A.B. degree *magna cum laude* in the Classics, and was elected a member of Phi Beta Kappa — a national American honor society which has as its motto *philosophia biou kybernetes*. He also received his A.M. (1953) and Ph.D. (1964) from Harvard University, and held an honorary Doctor of Letters degree from Hellenic College / Holy Cross Greek Orthodox School of Theology (1981).

---

* From *PLATON* (Athens), Vol. 45, Nos. 89-90, 1993.

He taught at Brandeis University in Waltham, Massachusetts, prior to joining the faculty at Colgate University in 1957. Since that year, he was on the Colgate faculty and served as Chairman of the Department of the Classics, Chairman of the Department of Classics, Slavic and Oriental Languages, Director of the Division of University Studies, Director of the Division of the Humanities, Associate Dean of the Faculty, and Acting Dean of the Faculty.

In the Fall Term 1972-1973, Dr. Rexine was Visiting Professor of Greek in the College Year in Athens program in Greece; and during 1979-1980, a Senior Fulbright Research Scholar in Athens at the Gennadius Library.

From 1977 to the time of his death, he was Vice President of the Institute for Byzantine and Modern Greek Studies.

Prof. Rexine was editor of *The Classical Outlook*, associate editor of *The Greek Orthodox Theological Review*, and book review editor for *Athene, The Modern Language Journal, The Hellenic Chronicle, The Orthodox Observer*, and *The Patristic and Byzantine Review*.

He authored the monograph *Solon and His Political Theory* (New York, 1958), and the books *Religion in Plato and Cicero* (New York, 1959), *The Hellenic*

Spirit: Byzantine and Post-Byzantine (Belmont, Massachusetts, 1981), and *An Explorer of Realms of Art, Life, and Thought: A Survey of the Works of Philosopher and Theologian Constantine Cavarnos* (Belmont, Massachusetts, 1985). In addition, he contributed chapters to several other books, and wrote numerous articles and over a thousand reviews.

His activities included participation in the following Professional Organizations: The American Philological Association, The Mediaeval Academy of America, The American Classical League, The Classical Association of the Atlantic States, and The Classical Association of the Empire State, which he served as President from 1987 to 1990.

He is listed in *Who's Who in the World*, and *Who's Who in America.*

The Oecumenical Patriarchate of Constantinople, recognizing Dr. Rexine's significant contributions to making the Orthodox Christian Faith better known in the world, honored him in 1967 with the offikion of *Didaskalos tou Genous.* For the same contributions he was awarded in 1992 in America the Florovsky Theological Prize, which he shared jointly with Dr. Constantine Cavarnos.

Prof. John E. Rexine was a first rate scholar, the foremost Greek-American classicist of recent years. He has been aptly characterized by one of his colleagues at Colgate University as "an adornment of his profession" (*The Colgate Scene*, July 1992, p. 5). He was not only a scholar of international renown, but also a noble and good man, a type of person called by the ancient Greeks *kalokágathos*, and an exemplary Christian.

PART I

PHILOSOPHICAL WORKS

THE HELLENIC-CHRISTIAN PHILOSOPHICAL TRADITION

Four Lectures delivered at Boston University.
An original discussion of the Legacy of Socrates,
Plato and Aristotle in the Hellenic East
from ancient to modern times, of Stoic elements
in the Greek Church Fathers, and of the
Concept of Philosophy in ancient Greece,
Byzantium, and modern Greece.

by

CONSTANTINE CAVARNOS, Ph.D.

With an Introduction by
PROFESSOR STEPHEN D. SALAMONE, Ph.D.,
of Boston University

INSTITUTE FOR BYZANTINE AND MODERN GREEK STUDIES
115 GILBERT ROAD
BELMONT, MASSACHUSETTS 02178 U.S.A.

1

*THE HELLENIC-CHRISTIAN PHILOSOPHICAL TRADITION**

The Hellenic-Christian Philosophical Tradition originally constituted four lectures presented at Boston University under the sponsorship of the Department of Classical Studies and the Program of Modern Greek Studies, the first three during the Spring of 1987 and "Aristotle's Legacy in the Hellenic East" in the Spring of 1988. The series was originally called "The Hellenic Philosophical Continuum," since the lectures were to focus on "the fact that there has been in the Hellenic East an uninterrupted stream of philosophical thought from antiquity to the present — a stream in which all the vital elements of the earlier stages of philosophy

* Published in *The Greek Orthodox Theological Review*, Vol. 35, No. 3, 1990, pp. 272, 274–276.

were retained, organically assimilated, refined, and enriched by that of later periods" (p. v).

Prof. Stephen Salamone is right in his Introduction that Dr. Cavarnos is one of very few professionals in the academic world who can focus on the *essence* of Hellenism, because he has studied Greek philosophy and culture from an *integrated standpoint*. Salamone calls Cavarnos' approach *essentialist* with "real potential for achieving a truly diachronic understanding of human nature and the evolution of human culture beyond the limitations of Western ethnocentrism" (p. 10). Salamone credits Cavarnos with generating "an anthropology that seeks to reestablish Greece at the center of contemporary humanist studies" (p. 9).

There is no doubt that *The Hellenic-Christian Philosophical Tradition* is a ground-breaking book that should have a profound impact upon how we look at the relation of Greek philosophy to Eastern Christianity. So much has been written of the impact and relation of Greek philosophy to Western culture and religion, but very little the other way around. Cavarnos' book sets for us briefly, concisely, and authoritatively the means for understanding "Plato's Legacy in the Hellenic

East;" "Aristotle's Legacy in the Hellenic East;" "Stoic Elements in the Greek Church Fathers;" and "The Concept of Philosophy in the Hellenic tradition" (the four titles of the four lectures which constitute the heart of this elegantly written book).

Plato is shown to have significantly contributed to Christianity through his distinction of the sensible and the intelligible realm; God as Demiourgos; his view of the human soul; the four general virtues (wisdom, courage, temperance, and justice); the unity of the virtues; and the beautiful.

Aristotle's legacy is discussed in terms of the distinction between matter and form; the notion of immaterial being; the conception of God; his ten categories (substance, quantity, quality, relation, place, time, position, state, action, and passion); his theory of moral excellence or virtue, virtues being qualities acquired through choices and deliberate actions, guided by *reason* and experience. The role of reason in the moral life is stressed by the Church Fathers, and practice and habituation are stated in Patristic writings as necessary for the acquisition of moral virtues. Cavarnos shows that not all of Aristotle was acceptable to the Church Fathers, but that they did use certain features of his philosophy.

In the case of Stoic philosophy, Cavarnos discusses (1) the governing principle of the human soul; (2) preconceptions; (3) examining the fantasies; (4) assent and refusal of assent; (5) relations; (6) tranquillity; and (7) freedom from passions. After giving us a review of the nature of Stoicism and comparison with terms and doctrines in the Greek Church Fathers, Dr. Cavarnos concludes that (1) The Church Fathers had no use for Stoic pantheism — for the Stoic view of Nature as the body of God and the human soul as part of God, destined to lose its individuality, its personal character after death, or for Stoic fatalism and belief in the periodic destruction and reconstitution of the universe; (2) the Church Fathers did adopt a number of Stoic terms; (3) Stoic and Christian doctrines denoted by most of these terms had certain similarities but also important differences; and (4) the Greek Fathers were very selective in their use of terms and ideas from Stoicism.

Probably the most important and best Chapter in Cavarnos' book is "The Concept of Philosophy in the Hellenic Tradition." It is a masterpiece of precision. In dealing with philosophy in Pre-Christian times, he beautifully shows how philosophy was viewed as (1) love of wisdom; (2) *meléte thanátou* (meditation practice on death); (3) self-examination and cross-examination; (4) dialectic; (5) the way of the best life; and (6) organized knowledge in general (Aristotle), plus four others described as (7) theoretical philosophy; (8) practical philosophy; (9) "first philosophy," theology, or metaphysics; and (10) physical philosophy. In the Christian period we find the distinction between (1) external and (2) internal philosophy; (3) Orthodox teaching as philosophy; (4) lived Christian teaching as philosophy; (5) the practices of inner attention and inner quiet as philosophy; and (6) the monastic way of life as philosophy.

The Hellenic-Christian Philosophical Tradition is an absolutely essential book for every serious student of the Hellenic tradition and of Orthodox Christianity. As Dr. Stephen Salamone has declared in his Introduction (p. 4), it is a work "which focuses on the *essence* of Hellenism, offers Greek and Western scholars an unparalleled opportunity and a challenge — that is, to rethink both sides of the relationship between Eastern and Western interpretations of the Hellenic Tradition" (*ibid.*). It is a book that demonstrates the historic relationship between philosophy and religion, and the necessity for looking at Greek religion and spirituality in its own terms, culturally and linguistically. Cavarnos' *Hellenic-Christian Philosophical Tradition* helps us enormously to understand the similarities and the difference of a common heritage.

2

MODERN GREEK THOUGHT
Second Edition*

Modern Greek Thought was originally published in 1969 and has now been reissued in the simple but handsome format that we have become familiar with from the Institute for Byzantine and Modern Greek Studies. It has not been updated. Still, Dr. Cavarnos has provided us with an unusual book about many of Greece's most prominent intellectuals (philosophers, theologians, scientists, poets, novelists, and others) from the middle of the eighteenth century to the present.

Modern Greek Thought is made up of three essays. The first is simply called "Philosophy" and discovers as the characteristics of modern Greek

---

* Published in *Diakonia*, Vol. XX, No. 3, 1986, pp. 179–181.

MODERN GREEK THOUGHT

THREE ESSAYS DEALING WITH
PHILOSOPHY, CRITIQUE OF SCIENCE,
AND VIEWS OF MAN'S NATURE AND DESTINY

BY

CONSTANTINE CAVARNOS

INSTITUTE FOR BYZANTINE
AND MODERN GREEK STUDIES
115 Gilbert Road
Belmont, Massachusetts

philosophy: (1) an existential orientation; (2) personalism ("personality is the highest value to which everything else is in principle subordinate"); (3) idealism or transcendentalism (with "the affirmation of a reality other than the material, physical world"); (4) the ranking of philosophy above science; (5) the ranking of Christian teaching above philosophy; (6) Christian eclecticism; (7) the use of ancient Greek philosophy as a preparatory discipline and the appropriation of many elements from it; (8) independence of mediaeval Western philosophy; (9) independence of the philosophy of the Middle and Far East. Dr. Cavarnos succinctly and brilliantly analyzes each of these characteristics and concludes that "modern Greek philosophy can best be understood as a continuation of Byzantine philosophy in modern times, a continuation which in general has preserved the existential orientation and distinctive Christian outlook of the Byzantines" (p. 37).

The second essay, "Critique of Science," examines science and general education; internal knowledge and scientific knowledge; scientific materialism; ethics and science; and religion and science. Scientism or negativistic Humanism is shown not to be acceptable to many Greek thinkers, and Nicholas Louvaris is cited as arguing that (1) scientific knowledge is not the only possible form of knowledge; (2) science is not in a position to regulate moral and political life; (3) science can neither prove nor refute the world of values and its truth.

Dr. Cavarnos' concluding essay on the "Views of Man's Nature and Destiny" follows quite naturally from the first two and really caps them. The importance of man; potential and actual being of man; soul and body; reason; conscience; the heart; the will; the imagination; the immortality of the soul; and the resurrection of the body. These are examined with respect to the role that they play in writers both religious and secular. And he emerges with a picture of modern Greek thought as essentially Greek Orthodox thought. Perhaps the quotation from Nikephoros Theotokis amply epitomizes this view: "Man is the most remarkable of all God's creatures. He is the creature that more than all others has manifested the infinite wisdom and power of God" (p. 57). The stress is on man's creation in the image and likeness of God, "an image of God as regards the soul, and a likeness of

God as regards the achievement of virtue" (*ibid.*). The final purpose of man's creation is viewed in terms of what the Byzantines called *théosis*, "man's deification, his union with God, his participation in God's perfection and blessedness" (p. 58).

The reader is left with the profound impression that modern Greek thought is essentially Christian in outlook, and specifically Orthodox in orientation. Some critics will no doubt dispute this, but they will be hard put to counter Dr. Cavarnos' well documented presentation. It is a presentation that will make for a better understanding of modern Greece and Orthodox spirituality, and will be a valuable source of illumination for students of ancient and Byzantine Greek civilization as well.

A DIALOGUE BETWEEN BERGSON, ARISTOTLE, AND PHILOLOGOS

A COMPARATIVE AND CRITICAL STUDY OF SOME ASPECTS OF HENRI BERGSON'S THEORY OF KNOWLEDGE AND OF REALITY

By

CONSTANTINE CAVARNOS

WITH A PREFACE BY JOHN WILD,
AN INTRODUCTION BY C. D. GEORGOULIS
AND COMMENTS BY C.I. LEWIS AND RAPHAEL DEMOS

Third, enlarged edition

INSTITUTE FOR BYZANTINE
AND MODERN GREEK STUDIES
115 Gilbert Road
Belmont, Massachusetts 02178
U.S.A.

3

A DIALOGUE BETWEEN BERGSON, ARISTOTLE, AND PHILOLOGOS
Third Edition*

*D*r. Constantine Cavarnos was trained at Harvard as a philosopher, and has taught philosophy, and has written on philosophical subjects. The publication of a third edition of *A Dialogue between Bergson, Aristotle, and Philologos*, is a good example of him at work as a philosopher. This third edition contains an introduction by a leading Greek philosopher and authority on Aristotle, C. D. Georgoulis (1894-1968), a photocopy of the two-page commentary by Professor Clarence Irving Lewis of Harvard, and one by Professor Raphael Demos, also of Harvard, a bibli-

---

* Published in *Diakonia*, Vol. XXI, No. 3, 1987, pp. 303-305.

ography, and indexes. The original was printed in 1949 and was the winner of a prestigious Bowdoin Prize at Harvard University in 1947. It was Dr. Cavarnos' "first book," a philosophical dialogue in which the basic and dominant questions are, according to Harvard Professor John Wild in the Preface: (1) "What is that ever present dynamism and change with which the whole world of nature is always pulsating?" (2) "What is that rational insight or awareness which is the peculiar possession of man?"

In this lively interchange of ideas, Bergson is very much the center of attention or, at least, argument. Bergson is represented as one whose interest in philosophy is purely theoretical, and not at all concerned with action or utility, who insists that reality can be known by intuition — intuition which apprehends the external world or matter ("pure perception"), and intuition which apprehends the internal world or spirit ("pure memory"). In the perception of external objects "we grasp ... at one and the same time, a 'state' of our consciousness and a 'reality' independent of ourselves. This mixed character of our immediate perception, this appearance of a realized contradiction is the principal theoretical reason that we have for believing in an external world which does not coincide absolutely with our perceptions."

Aristotle criticizes Bergson's view of perception as very subjectivistic, and reacts strongly to Bergson's statement that matter is "the aggregate of images and 'perception of matter' those images referred to the eventual action of one particular image, my body" (p. 36). He points out an abandonment of the distinction between mind and matter, and a reduction of everything to mind and the mental, either conscious or unconscious; and he accuses Bergson of idealism (the word is used here to mean mentalism) in the name of common sense.

Bergson counters by insisting that reality is fundamentally spiritual or mental: "Spirit is the movement of reality upward, matter is the movement of reality downward. Spirit is the tension of reality, the inextensive, heterogeneous movement which creates itself, it is the primal *vital impetus* itself. Matter, on the other hand, is the extension of the detention of the tension of life..." (p. 38).

Instead of perception, Bergson prefers the word "intuition" — that is, "instinct that has become disinterested and self-conscious, capable of reflecting, upon its object and enlarging upon it indefinitely" (p. 39).

Philologos gets concerned over Bergson's use of intuition as instinct capable of reflecting, intellectual as against non-intellectual, and is troubled that Bergson's "intuition" makes the senses theoretically and actually superfluous.

In order to clarify his position, Bergson sets out to discuss the intuition of spirit ("pure memory") which he finds similar to the intuition of matter, "in that by it one enters into the object, entirely overcomes externality and coincides with the object, dispensing entirely with concepts, with universals" (p. 41).

Then Aristotle points out that until the intellect has performed an act of abstraction ("the drawing out of the universal") upon sense perception and memory there can be no knowledge, and that the universal is in experience. He rejects Bergson's view that the intellect is incapable of grasping change — physical or psychical.

Philologos next takes issue with Bergson's view of the intellect as not at all a theoretical faculty, but one concerned with acting and producing or making. He tries to show that Bergson confuses theoretical with practical reason, depending too heavily on Kant's *Critique of Pure Reason* as definitive with regard to reason, and echoing Kant in what he says about the intellect and intellectual knowledge.

Later on, Bergson says that "reality itself, in the profoundest meaning of the word, is reached by the combined and progressive development of 'science,' which employs the intellect, and 'philosophy,' which employs intuition. Science is indispensable to philosophy" (p. 59).

Aristotle sees in Bergson's use of intuition his own use of induction, at one point. Bergson's "spirit of synthesis" he calls "the comparison of a form with other perfectly similar forms, seeing that the concept applies equally well to all" (p. 63). Aristotle insists upon structure being *in* reality and, with Philologos, believes that Bergson's theory of knowledge needs to be considerably modified to be persuasive. The epistemology of Bergson is held to be vitiated by a defective metaphysics, which subjectivizes structure.

In *A Dialogue between Bergson, Aristotle, and Philologos*, Dr. Cavarnos has skillfully used the dramatic dialogue to present us with the problems of change, knowledge, and structure of reality, by introducing us to two great philosophical figures.

PHOTIAN STUDIES

Edited by

George Papademetriou

HOLY CROSS ORTHODOX PRESS
Brookline, Massachusetts 02146

4

*SAINT PHOTIOS THE GREAT AS A PHILOSOPHER**

*I*n 1982 Hellenic College / Holy Cross Library began a tradition of celebrating the Feast of Saint Photios, Patriarch of Constantinople, as patron saint of its library. The celebration was accompanied by an annual lecture. Some of these lectures, like those in the present small volume, were published.

Photian Studies, in addition to Father Papademetriou's brief introduction, contains seven essays (lectures) of varying sizes, from Panagiotes Chrestou's two page statement on "Saint Photios as Preserver of Books" — itself an appropriate introduction to a series celebrating Photios as lover and writer of books — to Metropolitan Emilianos

---

* Published in *The Patristic and Byzantine Review*, Vol. 9, Nos. 2 and 3, 1990, pp. 204-206.

Timiades' longish (eighteen pages) and discursive paper on "Saint Photios on Transcendence of Culture." The latter hardly discusses Photios himself directly at all, but ranges over the theological history of East and West prior to Photios (it is really the story of how the East and the West grew apart theologically and historically), though he does poignantly remark that "Photios finds in Western Christianity an irresistible process of Latinization and the practice of universal authority by the bishop of Rome" (p. 52).

Father Stanley Samuel Harakas' brief article on "The Word, the Book, the Library," capitalizes on the specific occasion of the Photian celebration "to articulate a philosophy of education for our institution" (p. 5). It seeks to show by the example of Photios that "The holy Book and the book of natural knowledge are equally related here at Hellenic College and Holy Cross" (p. 11). These seek "to unite the two books into a mutually informing unity, unconfusedly, indivisibly, and inseparably" (p. 13).

Professor George Bebis, in his contribution entitled "Saint Photios as an Orthodox Theologian and Scholar," finds him "to be a pillar of the

Church, a defender of the Orthodox faith, and a peer of the Apostles." He remarks that Photios "embodies the spirit of the Fathers who preceded him, as well as the true liturgical experience of the Church" (p. 15).

Undoubtedly the most original and most valuable paper in the whole collection is that by Dr. Constantine Cavarnos on "Saint Photios the Great as a Philosopher," revealing as it does Photios' use and knowledge of Greek philosophy, particularly the organic assimilation in his thought of elements drawn from Plato, Aristotle, and Stoicism. Cavarnos clearly demonstrates the inadequacy of the work of such scholars as Basil Tatakis, C.D. Georgoulis, and Milton Anastos on the subject. He goes back to all the available original works of Photios himself to show that he was *selective* in his use of ancient philosophers, and unlike the misstatements of previous scholars, that "Photios preferred Aristotle's philosophy to that of Plato," he incontrovertibly demonstrates Photios' wide knowledge and use of Plato.

Cavarnos emphasizes that: "Chiefly, what makes Photios a philosopher — a very important philosopher — is not the creative use of such elements, but the following qualities of his mind, explicitly noted in this paper or inferable from what has been said: The thirst for truth, the great love of wisdom, evidenced by his astonishing erudition; intellectual acuteness and profoundness; objectivity; a disciplined way of thinking and expression; the "higher faith," the illuminated state that shines through his writings; and the great breadth and unity of his intellectual vision (p. 40).

Cavarnos' article alone is worth the price of the book.

*DOSTOIEVSKY'S PHILOSOPHY OF MAN**

*I*n the monograph *Dostoievsky's Philosophy of Man*, Cavarnos tries to show that Dostoievsky is concerned with individual men in all their complexity, but especially in the individual's relations to other men, to God, and to Satan, and to the ideas an individual accepts or rejects. He examines particularly Dostoievsky's *The Brothers Karamazov* and *Notes from Underground* for key ideas. Dostoievsky is shown to be concerned with man's consciousness or awareness and with the individual's power of free choice — freedom of the will — creativity, suffering, conscience, and love.

What Dr. Cavarnos concludes is that there is a striking but not accidental commonalty in Or-

---

* Published in *Diakonia*, Vol. XX, No. 3, 1986.

MONOGRAPHIC SUPPLEMENT SERIES
NUMBER II

DOSTOIEVSKY'S PHILOSOPHY OF MAN

by Constantine Cavarnos

CENTER FOR TRADITIONALIST ORTHODOX STUDIES
Etna, California 96027
1987

thodox anthropology and Dostoievsky's view of man. Both share the following: (1) a placing of the contemplative life above the active life, the life of outer action; (2) a stress on the value of consciousness, awareness, inner wakefulness (recalling the *népsis* and *prosoché* of the *Philokalia* and other books of Orthodox spirituality); (3) the attachment of much significance to suffering as a means of spiritual development; (4) the recognition of the existence in man of the power of free choice or free will; (5) the view that man is a creative being, whose creativity includes the development of the inner man through "work on one's self," through "relentless self discipline," called by the Eastern Fathers *áskesis* or *ergasía*; (6) the emphasis on Christian love as the highest virtue; (7) the distinguishing of three distinct human levels, called in Orthodox teaching the carnal (*sarkikós*), the natural (*psychikós*), and the spiritual (*pneumatikós*) man, and corresponding in general to Dostoievsky's first level, second level, and third level respectively; and (8) finally, both Orthodoxy and Dostoievsky assert the real possibility of the individual progressing from the lowest to the highest level, that is, to the truly spiritual.

DOSTOIEVSKY

ΚΩΝΣΤΑΝΤΙΝΟΥ ΚΑΒΑΡΝΟΥ

Καθηγητοῦ Πανεπιστημίου

ΣΥΝΑΝΤΗΣΕΙΣ ΜΕ ΤΟΝ ΚΟΝΤΟΓΛΟΥ

ΕΚΔΟΤΙΚΟΣ ΟΙΚΟΣ "ΑΣΤΗΡ„
ΑΛ. & Ε. ΠΑΠΑΔΗΜΗΤΡΙΟΥ
ΛΥΚΟΥΡΓΟΥ 10 — ΑΘΗΝΑΙ

CONSTANTINE CAVARNOS

MEETINGS
WITH
KONTOGLOU

*Enlightening, lively discussions on Byzantine
iconography and music, diverse writers, philosophers
and theologians, and contemporary events
and trends, between the author and
the great icon painter, writer, and philosopher
Photios Kontoglou*

INSTITUTE FOR BYZANTINE
AND MODERN GREEK STUDIES
115 Gilbert Road
Belmont, Massachusetts 02178

6

*MEETINGS WITH KONTOGLOU**

*M*eetings with Kontoglou (*Synantéseis me ton Kontoglou*) is the third book of Professor Cavarnos in which he concerns himself with Photios Kontoglou (1895-1965), remarkable artist who followed the Byzantine tradition of iconography, literary figure, religious writer, and Christian philosopher. He had dealt with Kontoglou earlier, in his books *Byzantine Sacred Art*, first published in 1957, and *Greece and Orthodoxy*, published in 1967.

His new book purports to be a biography of the man based on his diary (i.e., Cavarnos') kept during various visits and meetings with Kontoglou at his home and elsewhere. As such, it bears the marks of the close personal relations that these two individuals had from 1952 to 1965.

---

* Published in *St. Vladimir's Theological Quarterly*, Vol. 30, No. 2, 1986, pp. 176-177.

Cavarnos begins the story in 1920 and carries it down to Kontoglou's death in 1965. The strong Orthodox Christian character of Kontoglou emerges unmistakenly in the encounters — intellectual, social, and professional — that Cavarnos had each and every time he met with this remarkable exponent of the genuine Byzantine Orthodox tradition in the modern world.

Cavarnos' is not the usual biographical account. It is one in which a strong-minded, dedicated, and learned artist, who could have been just as well known as a literary figure, distinguished himself as the most important Orthodox iconographer of the twentieth century. Cavarnos brings out the thoughts of this painter about his own painting, about the Byzantine Orthodox literature, about contemporary art and artists, about contemporary authors and literature, about Christian theology and the Church.

Meetings with Kontoglou is an intimate portrait of a person who himself lived a committed Orthodox Christian life with his family to the very end, who was an example of what he believed in and a source of inspiration to iconographers and theologians alike. In him Dr. Cavarnos found a kindred spirit.

7

*NEW LIBRARY**

*A*nyone familiar with the four decades of publishing activity by Dr. Constantine P. Cavarnos, knows that his work has ranged over the entire continuum of the Hellenic tradition from antiquity to the present, with special emphasis on the Greek Orthodox tradition. The volume entitled *New Library* is the first in a proposed series of three volumes, named after the ninth century work of Saint Photios the Great called *Bibliothéke* (*Library*). It contains reviews and discussions of fifty-two book reviews written by him between 1948 and 1988. The particular focus, in his words, has been "to giving as far as possible a series of significant glimpses of the long Hellenic

---

* Published in *The Greek Orthodox Theological Review*, Vol. 35, No. 3, 1990, pp. 272–274.

NEW LIBRARY

VOLUME ONE

Reviews and discussions of over fifty Books of Modern
Greek, American, Russian and other writers pertaining to
Philosophy—Ancient, Byzantine and Modern Greek—,
Eastern Orthodox Christianity, Byzantine Art, and
Hellenism.

By

CONSTANTINE CAVARNOS

INSTITUTE FOR BYZANTINE
AND MODERN GREEK STUDIES
115 Gilbert Road
Belmont, Massachusetts 02178

philosophico-religious tradition, beginning with the Classical, pre-Christian period, continuing with the Byzantine, Christian era, and ending with the post-Byzantine or modern centuries" (p. v). All but seven reviews have previously been published in journals, books, or the Boston weekly newspaper *The Hellenic Chronicle*. This series will give the reader a very good notion of the vast influence of the Hellenic/Orthodox tradition from antiquity to the present.

In addition to an alphabetical listing of authors whose books are reviewed in *New Library*, and indexes of proper names and subjects, there is a preface which stresses that the series intends to make those reviews and discussions easily accessible to scholars and the general reading public. The seven sections of the book center on (1) Ancient Greek Philosophers; (2) Byzantium, Its Philosophy, Theology, and Art; (3) Modern Greek Philosophers; (4) Modern Greek Religious Writers; (5) Russian Writers; (6) Hellenic Communities in Greece and Abroad; and (7) Modern Greece.

Reviews of Russian writers' books of the nineteenth and twentieth centuries are included "because their thought has much in common with that of the modern Greek writers whose books are discussed, both being rooted, to a greater or lesser extent, in the Orthodox Christian tradition that has been bequeathed by Byzantium" (p. v).

New Library can provide much continuous fascinating reading and valuable information. It can also be used as a handy reference book. We look forward to the other volumes.

PART II

THEOLOGICAL WORKS

MODERN ORTHODOX SAINTS

1

ST. COSMAS AITOLOS

Great Missionary, Awakener, Illuminator, and holy Martyr of Greece. An account of his Life, Character and Message, including his teaching on God, Heaven and Hell, and his Prophecies, together with Selections from his Sermons.

By

CONSTANTINE CAVARNOS

Third Edition
Revised and considerably enlarged

INSTITUTE FOR BYZANTINE
AND MODERN GREEK STUDIES
115 Gilbert Road
Belmont, Massachusetts 02178
U.S.A.

SAINT COSMAS D'ETOLIE

HIEROMARTYR EGAL-AUX-APOTRES

1714 - 1779

par

Constantin CAVARNOS

Fête : 24 août

Monastère Orthodoxe Saint-Michel 47230 Lavardac

St. Cosmas the New,
the Aitolian

Drawing inspired by an old icon.

8

ST. COSMAS AITOLOS
Third Edition*

*T*he reissuance of *St. Cosmas Aitolos*, Volume 1 in the *Modern Orthodox Saints* series inaugurated by Dr. Cavarnos in 1971, is a happy sign of the success and value of the series. St. Cosmas Aitolos (1714-1779) was declared a saint by the Oecumenical Patriarchate of Constantinople on April 20, 1961. Dr. Cavarnos has described the saint as "undoubtedly the greatest missionary of modern Greece" and "the Father of the modern Greek nation, a man who played a role of supreme importance in the moral and religious awakening and enlightenment of the Greeks during the second half of the eighteenth century, and thus more than

---

* Published in *St. Vladimir's Theological Quarterly*, Vol. 30, No. 2, 1986, pp. 177–178.

anyone else inaugurated the modern Greek era" (p. 13). Also described as "the Missionary of the Balkans," St. Cosmas Aitolos' work extended to Constantinople, Albania, and South Serbia, as well as Greece. The third edition of this beautifully produced volume has been considerably enlarged and revised: It has added: (1) the Apolytikion, Kontakion and Megalynarion of St. Cosmas, taken from the service composed in his honor by the eminent hymnographer Gerasimos Micragiannanitis of the Small Skete of St. Anna on Mount Athos; (2) a page of sayings regarding the "Value of Reading Lives of Saints;" (3) two essays: "On God" and "On Heaven and Hell," written by Dr. Cavarnos; (4) a chapter containing some of the "Prophecies of the Saint;" and (5) a "Selected Bibliography."

As in the original edition, so in the new one, an introductory essay provides the reader with the main outlines of the saint's life, character, and teaching. The translation of "The Life of Saint Cosmas," written by the saint's disciple Sapphiros Christodoulidis, augments our knowledge of this saint, while selections from his teaching bring us into intimate contact with the saint's thinking.

Particularly impressive is his emphasis on Love: "Fortunate is the man who has these two loves in his heart, that for God and that for his brethren. He surely has God; and whoever has God has every blessing and does not bear to commit sin" (p. 83).

4

ST. NIKEPHOROS OF CHIOS

Outstanding Writer of Liturgical Poetry and Lives of Saints, Educator, Spiritual Striver, and Trainer of Martyrs. An account of his Life, Character and Message, together with a Comprehensive List of his Publications, Selections from them, and Brief Biographies of eleven Neomartyrs and other Orthodox Saints who are treated in his works

By

CONSTANTINE CAVARNOS

INSTITUTE FOR BYZANTINE
AND MODERN GREEK STUDIES
115 Gilbert Road
Belmont, Massachusetts 02178
U.S.A.

9

ST. NIKEPHOROS OF CHIOS
Second Edition*

The original edition of this very handsomely produced book was published in 1976. The present edition contains everything the first edition contained, plus English translations of the Apolytikion, Kontakion, and Megalynarion in honor of Saint Nikephoros of Chios that appear at the beginning of the book; a photograph of one of the earliest icons depicting the saint; an additional select passage from his prose writings; and corrections of typographical errors.

Dr. Cavarnos again demonstrates for us the vitality of the series on *Modern Orthodox Saints* that he inaugurated in 1971. He has filled a dire

---

* Published in *The Greek Orthodox Theological Review*, Vol. 32, No. 3, 1987, p. 311.

ST. NIKEPHOROS OF CHIOS

Panel icon. Ca. 1907. Church of Hypapanti,
Upper Kardamyla, Chios.

need for such a series in the English-speaking world, and the reissuing of Volume 4 on Saint Nikephoros of Chios (1750-1821) is only the most recent example of this demand. Dr. Cavarnos provides the preface and introductory material on the saint, a translation of "The Life of St. Nikephoros by Emily Sarou;" a comprehensive list of the works of the saint; selected passages from his prose works; an anthology of his poetry; notes; brief biographies of eleven modern martyrs whom Saint Nikephoros mentions; a selected bibliography; and an index.

Saint Nikephoros, consistently Orthodox in his thoughts and his actions, sees as primary the development of the virtues, by which man achieves likeness to God, through which *theosis* (divinization) is attained. Union with God is thus man's ultimate aim, being a participation in God's perfection and glory. Blessedness through Divine grace is viewed as man's highest goal and one that characterizes the lives of the saints.

Though Saint Nikephoros never left Chios, his influence and reputation have gone well beyond the island. His life and works will no doubt interest students of the cultural and religious history of

Greece during the period of Ottoman Turkish occupation, as well as those concerned with Orthodox Christian spirituality.

MODERN ORTHODOX SAINTS

7

ST. NECTARIOS OF AEGINA

Metropolitan of Pentapolis, great Theologian, Philosopher, Moralist, Educator, Ascetic, Mystic, Miracle-Worker and Healer. An account of his Life, Character, Message and Miracles, together with a Comprehensive List of his Writings, Selections from them, and an Essay on his teaching on God.

By

CONSTANTINE CAVARNOS

Second Edition

INSTITUTE FOR BYZANTINE
AND MODERN GREEK STUDIES
115 Gilbert Road
Belmont, Massachusetts 02178
U.S.A.

St. Nectarios of Aegina

10

ST. NECTARIOS OF AEGINA

Second Edition*

Dr. Constantine Cavarnos has already presented to the reading public the most extensive
series of modern orthodox saints published in
English anywhere. So far volumes have been issued
about St. Cosmas Aitolos, St. Macarios of Corinth,
St. Nicodemos the Hagiorite, St. Nikephoros of
Chios, St. Seraphim of Sarov, St. Arsenios of
Paros, St. Nectarios of Aegina, St. Savvas the New
(of Kalymnos), and St. Methodia of Kimolos. A
number have been reprinted one or more times. The
St. Nectarios of Aegina volume is the most
recently reissued volume in the series, having been

---

* *Diakonia*, Vol. XXI, No. 3, 1987, pp. 201-203.

originally circulated in 1981. It is beautifully reproduced.

Nectarios Kephalas, Metropolitan of Pentapolis (1846-1920), founded the Holy Trinity Convent on the island of Aegina, where he lived a monastic life from 1908 to 1920. In his book, Dr. Cavarnos seeks "to give an account, not only of St. Nectarios' life and some of his miracles, but also of the nature and scope of the more than thirty books and the many pamphlets and articles which he published" (p. vii). In addition, he presents an extensive anthology from these on diverse topics, and an essay in which he highlights and summarizes the saint's important teaching about God.

Cavarnos' effort is one that began almost three decades ago, and contributed to his becoming more and more knowledgeable about the life, character, and thought of St. Nectarios. The reissued volume constitutes the first to have been published in English or in any language other than Greek. Though more than a dozen books on St. Nectarios have circulated in Greek, they can be generally characterized as biographical, laudatory, and concerned primarily with his miracles. His reputation as a miracle-worker, particularly as a healer of every kind of disease, undoubtedly contributed to this emphasis. Dr. Cavarnos points out that St. Nectarios was also a prolific writer, theologian, moralist, educator, poet, ascetic, and mystic.

As the most widely known Greek Orthodox saint after Sts. Cosmas Aitolos and Nicodemos the Hagiorite, according to Cavarnos, "the extent and character of the writings of St. Nectarios place him among the great educators, moralists, and religious philosophers of modern Greece, and among the holy Fathers and Teachers of the Orthodox Church" (p. 74).

The St. Nectarios volume is organized in much the same manner as the other volumes in the *Modern Orthodox Saints* series. The Apolytikion, Kontakion, and Megalynarion of the saint precede the main body of the work. After the Preface, there is an extensive and illuminating Introduction by the author (pp. 11-85); a translation of "The Life of St. Nectarios" by his student and friend Joachim Spetsieris (pp. 86-104); "Miracles of the Saint," including personal testimonials from people who were cured by him (pp. 105-116); "Works of the Saint" — an impressive bibliography of books authored, books edited, books put into verse, pamphlets, articles, letters and unpublished works (pp. 117-129); a substantial essay "On God" by Dr. Cavarnos, which includes citations from St. Nectarios (pp. 130-153); "Selected Passages from the Writings of the Saint" (pp. 154-187); "Notes" (pp. 188-205); "Bibliography" (pp. 206-210); and an "Index" (pp. 211-222).

Cavarnos' book gives us a very clear picture of St. Nectarios, especially of the way in which his life, work, and thought were characterized by his love of God. As the saint himself said, "Love of God is knowledge of God, for one who loves, loves what one has come to know, and it is impossible for one to love what is unknown.... Love of God expresses the yearning to be united with God as the supreme good" (p. 177).

St. Nectarios' life and conduct are eloquently characterized by the following passage by Archimandrite Joachim Spetsieris:

"His whole life was nothing else than a continuous doxology to God, and a tireless effort and assiduous concern to benefit suffering society morally and religiously. He lived *in* the world, but was *not*, as the Savior says, *of* the world. He trod on the earth, yet conducted himself like a citizen of heaven. He had the form of a man, but lived like an angel. He was clothed with flesh, but was a strict keeper and guardian of chastity. He associated with various kinds of persons, but spoke as a spiritual man, alien to the present world. He was transported by sublime ideals and warmed by the aspiration for moral perfection; and hence he abided in a state of inner calm and blessedness. His was a peace-making holiness, inspired by evangelical virtue and meditation on the eternal Kingdom of God" (p. 104).

St. Nectarios of Aegina is a splendid addition to the volumes in the series *Modern Orthodox Saints*. It deserves to be in the library of every institution concerned with or interested in the history, work, and thought of the Orthodox Church. It shows that Orthodox spirituality is still at work.

9

ST. METHODIA OF KIMOLOS

Remarkable Ascetic, Teacher of Virtue, Counselor, Comforter and Healer (1865–1908). An account of her Life, Character, Miracles and Influence, together with Selected Hymns from the Akolouthia in honor of her, and a Letter to her sister Anna.

By

CONSTANTINE CAVARNOS

INSTITUTE FOR BYZANTINE
AND MODERN GREEK STUDIES
115 Gilbert Road
Belmont, Massachusetts 02178
U.S.A.

11

*ST. METHODIA OF KIMOLOS**

St. Methodia is described as the most remarkable woman saint of recent times. A native of the tiny Cycladic island of Kimolos, she began her monastic life at the age of 17, and distinguished herself as a nun until her death at the age of 43 in 1908. She engaged in the traditional Eastern Orthodox monastic practices of long day and night prayers, meditation, study of religious writings, fasting and other forms of religious *askesis*. Thereby she developed into a person of exemplary virtue, a teacher of ideal Christian life, a counselor, comforter, and healer. She lived the life of an *énkleistos* (recluse) in an *énkleistron* (enclosure or hut).

---

* Published in *Diakonia*, Vol. XX, No. 3, 1986, pp. 177-178.

ST. METHODIA

Photograph.

THE THEOTOKOS AS HODEGETRIA

Detail of an old panel icon in the Church of St. John
Chrysostom in Kimolos as drawn by Photios Kontoglou *ca.*
1928. See the Appendix, pp. 109–110.)

In keeping with the practice established in his other volumes, Dr. Cavarnos provides the reader with a Preface and an Introductory in which he tries to give us as complete a picture of St. Methodia as is possible in the light of the information available. This includes an overview of her life, character, thought, and the influence that she exercised in Kimolos and elsewhere in Greece, and also the recognition of her sainthood. He has used as sources the biography and *akolouthia* written by Father Gerasimos Micragiannanitis in 1962 and 1947 respectively, the biography authored by Emmanuel I. Karpathios in 1947, and Athena Karampetsou's book *Three Women Saints of Our Century*, published in 1985, and other publications.

Having translated *The Life of St. Methodia of Kimolos* by Gerasimos Micragiannanitis of Mount Athos, Cavarnos has had it follow his Introductory in this book. Then follow "Selected Hymns from the Akolouthia of St. Methodia;" "Scriptural Texts from the Akolouthia of St. Methodia That Help Us Understand Her Life Better;" "A Letter of St. Methodia to Her Sister Anna;" "Sayings of St. Methodia;" "Notes;" an Appendix on "Kimolos" by Photios Kontoglou; a Bibliography and an Index.

He has also included a map showing Kimolos and the other Cyclades islands, a diagram of the fortress inside which was the saint's hermitage, illustrations of some of the churches of Kimolos associated with her life and of some old icons in the Byzantine tradition, a photograph of St. Methodia, and three photographs of icons portraying her.

All this rich material makes available in English for the first time a Greek Orthodox nun who in her life reflected "the highest of the Christian virtues: love of God, reflected in her frequent references to His name and her total commitment to Him; and love of her fellowmen, manifested in her prayers for the living and the dead, her compassion and affection for people, and her eagerness to help the poor and the ill.... The *askesis* of the holy Mother also resulted in the gifts of spiritual knowledge and understanding, and that of spiritual healing. These gifts, together with the virtues just mentioned, made her a very successful spiritual teacher, counselor, and comforter" (p. 142).

10

SAINTS RAPHAEL, NICHOLAS AND IRENE OF LESVOS

Newly manifested Saints, who suffered Martyrdom by the Ottoman Turks in 1463 at the Monastery of the Nativity of the Theotokos near the village of Thermi on the Island of Lesvos. An account of their Life, Character, Message, and Miracles.

By

CONSTANTINE CAVARNOS

INSTITUTE FOR BYZANTINE
AND MODERN GREEK STUDIES
115 Gilbert Road
Belmont, Massachusetts 02178
U.S.A.

12

SAINTS RAPHAEL,
*NICHOLAS, AND IRENE**

Constantine Cavarnos inaugurated the *Modern Orthodox Saints* series in 1971. In the two decades since then, ten volumes have appeared. When one considers the span of time and the range of subject matter, this is a truly remarkable achievement and a major contribution in English to Orthodox Christian hagiography. The appearance of the tenth volume, devoted to Saints Raphael, Nicholas, and Irene, is an appropriate occasion on which to congratulate their author, Constantine Cavarnos, for his dedication and selflessness to a most worthy cause and to a project that is unique in its high significance and long-term value.

---

* Published in *St. Vladimir's Theological Quarterly*, Vol. 35, No. 4, 1991, pp. 410-412.

STS. RAPHAEL, NICHOLAS, AND IRENE

The tenth volume in the *Modern Orthodox Saints* series is dedicated to three newly revealed saints who suffered martyrdom at the hands of the Ottoman Turks in 1463 at the Monastery of the Nativity of the Theotokos near the village of Thermi on the island of Lesvos, ten years after the fall of the Byzantine imperial capital to the Turks. Dr. Cavarnos explains that he has included these chronologically earlier saints in his series at this time because they were unknown until 1959. He himself visited the site of Karyes in 1961 where the martyrdom took place. He interviewed the principal persons who claimed to have seen the saints in dreams and visions, spent time in Karyes and Thermi, and gathered much material. This was supplemented by material from the book *A Great Sign (Semeíon Méga)* by the noted iconographer and writer Photios Kontoglou (first published in 1962), and others.

The current book is organized in a fashion similar to the others in the series. Cavarnos provides an Introductory that is followed by translations of hymnographer Gerisimos Micragrannanitis' "Life of Saints Raphael, Nicholas, and Irene;" "Miraculous Cures (1959-1961)" by Photios

Kontoglou; "Miraculous Cures (1959-1967)" by Iakovos Kleomvrotos, Metropolitan of Mytilene; "Miraculous Cures (1969-1984)" as narrated by persons who became well or by their relatives; "Spiritual Counsels of St. Raphael;" "Lessons We Learn from the Saints of Thermi" by Constantine Cavarnos; and "Reflections on the Appearances of the Saints" by Photios Kontoglou, followed by Notes, Bibliography, and Index. There is also a Preface, the Apolytikia, Kontakion, and Megalynarion in honor of these martyrs.

A great deal of the book is dedicated to the dreams, visions, and healing of people who experienced the presence of the saints and their benefaction, and to the discovery and excavation of the site of their martyrdom.

Cavarnos himself believes that we can draw certain conclusions from these revelations. One of the conclusions is that "there is such a thing as *psyche* or *soul* — an entity distinct from the body, an enduring center of consciousness, of thinking, of feeling, of choosing or willing, of distinguishing between truth and falsehood, good and evil, the beautiful and the ugly — an entity, often spoken of as "the inner man, which survives the death of the body, is immortal" (p. 156); that the God of believers "is a God of the living, not of the dead, for all live unto Him." Other conclusions are that the manifestations of these saints confirm the Church's teaching of the intercession of saints, and that "their relics are channels of Divine grace, and hence should be looked upon and treated with great reverence" (p. 161). In connection with the last, he cites St. Symeon the New Theologian and Nicholas Cavasilas, and the Orthodox doctrine of *theosis* or the divinization of man through Divine grace.

Additionally, he emphasizes the significance of holy martyrdom — of enduring tortures and death for one's religious faith. He states that through martyrdom, the martyr becomes a recipient of Divine grace, is purified of all taint of sin and is sanctified, receiving heavenly glory and honor. Also, through martyrdom, faith is revitalized in people" (p. 166). He also points out that the appearances of the Martyrs of Thermi reaffirm the teaching of the Orthodox Church that miraculous cures are effected by the saints during their lifetime and after their death. And he notes that the counsels of these newly martyred saints stress the importance of the virtues of faith, obedience to

God, humility, patience, spiritual love and forgiveness, and the practices of repentance, fasting, confession, Holy Communion, the reading of religious books, and prayer.

Constantine Cavarnos has now made it possible for a much wider audience to learn about these saints and the lessons that can be learned from them by Orthodox Christians everywhere.

13

*THE SIGNIFICANCE OF THE NEW MARTYRS**

The Significance of the New Martyrs in the Life of the Orthodox Church outlines the categories of saints (martyrs, apostles, prophets, hierarchs, monastics [*hósioi*], and the righteous [*díkaioi*]. Each of these categories represents a *way* for Christians to attain *théosis*, to become saints. The martyr becomes holy through repentance and confession, fasting, vigil, unceasing prayer, partaking of Holy Communion, and confessing the Orthodox Christian faith before anti-Christian tyrants and executioners.

The way of the martyr is open to all at all times in all places, when personal circumstances recommend it. The New Martyrs are dated from the

---

* Published in *The Patristic and Byzantine Review*, Vol. 13, Nos. 1, 2, 3, 1994, p. 142.

MONOGRAPHIC SUPPLEMENT SERIES
NUMBER IV

CONSTANTINE CAVARNOS

THE SIGNIFICANCE OF THE NEW MARTYRS
IN THE LIFE OF THE ORTHODOX CHURCH

Translated from the Greek by
Patrick G. Barker

CENTER FOR TRADITIONALIST
ORTHODOX STUDIES
Etna, California 96027
1992

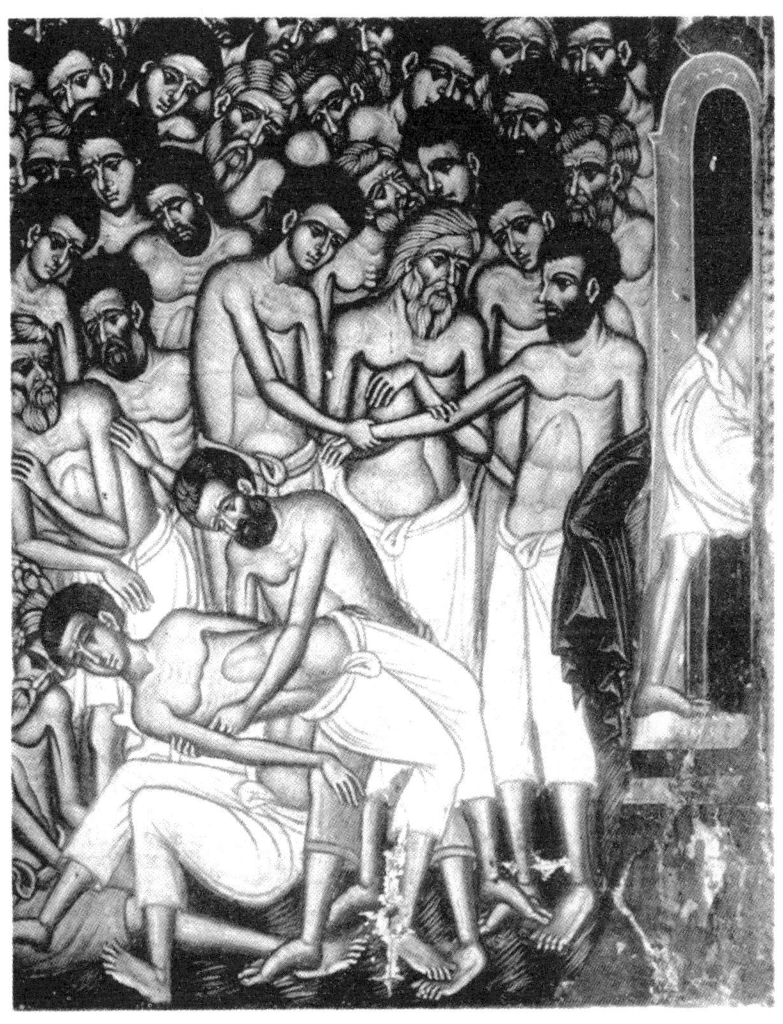

The Forty Martyrs. Detail. XV-XVIth century. Panel icon, Byzantine Museum, Athens.

Fall of Constantinople in 1453 and are numbered in the thousands.

Dr. Cavarnos enumerates and explains in detail the various kinds of significance which the lives of the new martyrs have in the Orthodox Church. For example, they constitute a confutation and negation of heretics, a justification of the Orthodox Church, and an encouragement and incitement for all Christians. The point is strongly made that martyrs are not limited to any chronological period.

ΚΩΝΣΤΑΝΤΙΝΟΥ ΚΑΒΑΡΝΟΥ
Καθηγητοῦ Πανεπιστημίου

Η ΟΡΘΟΔΟΞΟΣ ΠΑΡΑΔΟΣΙΣ ΚΑΙ Ο ΣΥΓΧΡΟΝΙΣΜΟΣ

ΕΚΔΟΣΕΙΣ
«ΟΡΘΟΔΟΞΟΥ ΤΥΠΟΥ»
ΑΘΗΝΑΙ 1971

MONOGRAPHIC SUPPLEMENT SERIES
NUMBER V

CONSTANTINE CAVARNOS

ORTHODOX TRADITION AND MODERNISM

Translated from the Greek by
Patrick G. Barker

CENTER FOR TRADITIONALIST
ORTHODOX STUDIES
Etna, California 96027
1992

14

*ORTHODOX TRADITION AND MODERNISM**

*O*rthodox Tradition and Modernism was originally delivered as a lecture in Athens for the Panhellenic Orthodox Union in May of 1970. It deals with the questions of what Sacred Tradition is; what validity does it have; what its relation is to the Orthodox Church; how it is viewed by the heterodox; and the relation of Tradition to the Holy Synods and to the Church Fathers.

Using Biblical, Patristic, hagiographic, theological, and recent scholarly sources, Cavarnos pinpoints various attempts at "modernization" from the eighteenth century to the present. The two parts of Tradition (oral and written) are carefully explored. He stresses that "It is to the Synods and

------

* Published in *The Patristic and Byzantine Review*, Vol. 13, Nos. 1, 2, 3, 1994, p. 142.

to the holy Fathers that we owe the preservation and guarding of Sacred Tradition, which the Lord gave, and the Apostles proclaimed, and upon which the Orthodox Church is founded" (p. 15).

ΚΩΝΣΤΑΝΤΙΝΟΥ ΚΑΒΑΡΝΟΥ
ΚΑΘΗΓΗΤΟΥ ΠΑΝΕΠΙΣΤΗΜΙΟΥ

ΤΟ ΖΗΤΗΜΑ ΤΗΣ ΕΝΩΣΕΩΣ

ΠΡΟΛΟΓΟΣ ΚΑΙ ΕΙΚΟΝΕΣ
Ὑπὸ ΦΩΤΙΟΥ Ν. ΚΟΝΤΟΓΛΟΥ

ΕΚΔΟΣΕΙΣ
"ΟΡΘΟΔΟΞΟΥ ΤΥΠΟΥ„
ΑΘΗΝΑΙ 1968

CONSTANTINE CAVARNOS

THE QUESTION
OF UNION

A forthright discussion of the possibility of union of the Eastern Orthodox Church and Roman Catholicism

**Translated by
Patrick Barker**

With a Preface by Photios Kontoglou
and Foreword by
Bishop Chrysostomos

CENTER FOR TRADITIONALIST
ORTHODOX STUDIES
Etna, California 96027
1992

15

*THE QUESTION OF UNION**

$\mathcal{D}$r. Constantine Cavarnos, President of the Institute for Byzantine and Modern Greek Studies, a *magna cum laude* graduate of Harvard College with an A.M. and Ph.D. from Harvard University in Philosophy, and wide experience as a college and university teacher, is a prolific author and publisher of books on Byzantine and Orthodox Christian subjects, and perhaps the most respected lay expert on Greek Orthodox ascetical theology and hagiography in the Western world. The fact that the Center for Traditional Orthodox Studies has seen fit to translate and reprint a number of his works would seem to be a fit tribute to the extensive contributions that he has made for a better understanding of the Orthodox Church, its tra-

---

* Published in *The Patristic and Byzantine Review*, Vol. 13, Nos. 1, 2, 3, 1994, pp. 141-142.

ditions, its beliefs, its practices, and its relations with the heterodox. All his works exhibit his ability to present his subject matter precisely, directly, and clearly in a straightforward but civil manner.

The Question of Union, originally published in Greek in 1964 by the "Orthodox Press" of Athens (Second Greek language edition in 1968) remains the single best summary of the key differences between Greek Orthodoxy and Roman Catholicism in language and style that any lay-person can understand. Dr. Cavarnos notes the dogmatic differences of the primacy and infallibility of the Pope, the *filioque*, purgatory, and the immaculate conception of the Holy Virgin Mary — all unacceptable to the Orthodox — and the sacramental differences in baptism (immersion and emersion vs. aspertion); the use of unleavened vs. leavened bread in the Divine Liturgy; the fact that the Roman Church does not offer the Chalice in "both species" to the faithful; sanctification of the Holy Gifts offered not through the invocation (*epíklesis*); and the restricted use of the *Evchélaion* or sacrament of Unction. In worship, Dr. Cavarnos notes the extensive use of statues by the Roman Catholic Church vs. characteristic icons in the Orthodox

Church, and the much more worldly spirit of Rome (with the powerful historical examples of the Crusades and the Inquisition).

An appendix contains a Declaration of Faith by Patriarch Diodoros of Jerusalem made in 1992 on the Sunday of Orthodoxy and recorded in the minutes of the assembly of Orthodox hierarchs at the Phanar.

All in all, Cavarnos presents us with a magnificent summary of the traditionalist Orthodox position that clearly pinpoints the differences between Roman Catholicism and Greek Orthodoxy with a realistic assessment of the possibilities of a re-union between the two Churches.

MONOGRAPHIC SUPPLEMENT SERIES
NUMBER VII

CONSTANTINE CAVARNOS

FATHER GEORGES FLOROVSKY
on Ecumenism

CENTER FOR TRADITIONALIST
ORTHODOX STUDIES
Etna, California 96027
1992

16

*FATHER GEORGES FLOROVSKY ON ECUMENISM**

*F*or Father Florovsky, the contemporary Ecumenist has two goals, the *immediate* and the *ultimate*: (a) "To do away with our prejudices and our short-sightedness, to come closer to understanding the true meaning of the existing divisions and their real roots and causes" (p. 8), and (b) to bring about a practical cooperation among the various Christian groups, agreement on secular issues and how to address them. Christian *reunion* is for *him* simply universal conversion to Orthodoxy — to the Nicene Creed along with the formal definitions of the Seven Ecumenical Synods, with the Church's unbroken tradition. These provide "a true unanimity and ultimate identity of Faith" (p. 10).

---

* Published in *The Patristic and Byzantine Review*, Vol. 13, Nos. 1, 2, 3, 1994, p. 143.

FATHER GEORGES FLOROVSKY

(1893-1979)

Father Florovsky insisted that a comprehensive *doctrinal* agreement had to have priority, and that this involves teaching the Orthodox faith, which is "missionary activity" for the Orthodox in their participation in the Ecumenical Movement. "Maximalism" must be the approach for unity, and this for Florovsky means unity of faith, of life and love. Faith is to be taken seriously, to be regarded as the only truth that leads to salvation.

The Center for Traditionalist Orthodox Studies has done a distinct service for all Orthodox Christians and for all students of contemporary Orthodox Christianity by making available this and other studies by Dr. Cavarnos in a handy format. They can be readily used for personal or professional purposes, no matter what the jurisdictional loyalty or confessional allegiance of the individual.

ΚΩΝΣΤΑΝΤΙΝΟΥ Π. ΚΑΒΑΡΝΟΥ

Καθηγητοῦ Πανεπιστημίου

ΝΗΣΤΕΙΑ ΚΑΙ ΕΠΙΣΤΗΜΗ

Πραγματεία εἰς τὴν ὁποίαν συγκρίνονται ἡ Ἐπιστημονικὴ καὶ ἡ Ὀρθόδοξος Χριστιανικὴ Νηστεία ὡς πρὸς τὰς βάσεις, τοὺς σκοπούς, τὰς μεθόδους καὶ τὰ ἀποτελέσματά των, μαζὶ μὲ ἕνα Θησαύρισμα σχετικῶν χωρίων σταχυολογημένων ἀπὸ τὰ συγγράμματα ἀρχαίων καὶ νεωτέρων Ἰατρῶν καὶ Φιλοσόφων, τὴν Παλαιὰν καὶ Καινὴν Διαθήκην καὶ ἀπὸ κείμενα τῶν ἁγίων Ἀποστόλων, Πατέρων τῆς Ἐκκλησίας καὶ Ὑμνογράφων.

ΕΚΔΟΣΕΙΣ "ΟΡΘΟΔΟΞΟΥ ΤΥΠΟΥ„

ΚΑΝΙΓΓΟΣ 10, 10677, ΑΘΗΝΑΙ 1988

17

*FASTING AND SCIENCE**

*T*he main substance of this publication was originally delivered as a lecture to the Plomarion Club "Benjamin of Lesvos" on April 15, 1984, Palm Sunday. It was subsequently published serially in the Athenian religious newspaper *Orthodox Press* on April 4th, 11th, 18th, 25th, and May 2nd, 1986. Then it was translated into English by the Center for Traditionalist Orthodox Studies in Etna, California, and appeared in the periodical *Orthodox Tradition*, Vol. 5, Nos. 1, 2, and 3, 1988. Now it reappears in Greek in the form of a book for the first time, with the addition of selections of passages on fasting from ancient and contemporary physicians and philosophers, the Old and New Testaments, and from the texts of the Apostles, the

---

* Published in *The Greek Orthodox Theological Review*, Vol. 34, No. 4, 1989, pp. 407-408.

MONOGRAPHIC SUPPLEMENT SERIES
NUMBER III

FASTING AND SCIENCE

A Study of the Scientific Support and
Patristic Foundation for Fasting
in the Orthodox Church

by

CONSTANTINE CAVARNOS

Translated from the Greek

by

Bishop Chrysostomos
and Hieromonk Auxentios

CENTER FOR TRADITIONALIST ORTHODOX
STUDIES
Etna, California 96027
1988

Church Fathers, and hymnographers. It forms a compact volume bringing together scientific and religious views on the practice of fasting. It is especially useful in this age of special diets, special foods, and exercise plans.

What Dr. Cavarnos has sought to do in this work is to compare the bases, purposes, methods, and results of fasting according to the religious practices and traditions of the Greek Orthodox faith, with those according to science. His comparison and bibliography reveal some practices and purposes that both hold in common. The scientists are interested in promoting the good health of the body; religion, the good health of the soul as well as the body. Whether it is the one-meal-a-day or two-meals-a-day plan, each recommends limitations of one's diet in terms of intake and in terms of the kind of food that is ingested: "The Orthodox Church justifies fasts that involve the abstinence from certain foods and reduction of the amount of food eaten on certain days and during certain periods. The medical profession . . . reduces the quantity of food to nothing for a restricted period of time, in order to give the organism the opportunity to accomplish its own detoxification" (p. 30).

Dr. Cavarnos includes in his collection of citations a particularly apt quotation from Saint Symeon the New Theologian that reinforces his main text:

"Fasting, which is the physician of our souls, is conducive, in the case of one Christian to humbling his flesh; of another, to soothing his anger. From one it drives away torpor and to another it brings the desire to do good. Of one it clears his mind, and liberates him from evil thoughts. Of one it subdues his untamed and uncontrollable tongue . . . and of another it keeps his eyes from looking here and there, and busying themselves with what others are doing. It makes each one pay attention to himself and to remember his own sins and faults. Fasting gradually refines the covering of sin which is over our soul, and drives from it the mental darkness, just as the sun drives away the fog. Fasting makes us see clearly the spiritual atmosphere, in which always shines the spiritual Sun of Justice, our Lord Jesus Christ" (p. 73).

It is ultimately Cavarnos' goal to demonstrate the value of fasting for body and soul, that it plays an organic role in Orthodox Christian life, bound as it is inextricably with the practice of faith, prayer, charity, discretion, and every other virtue.

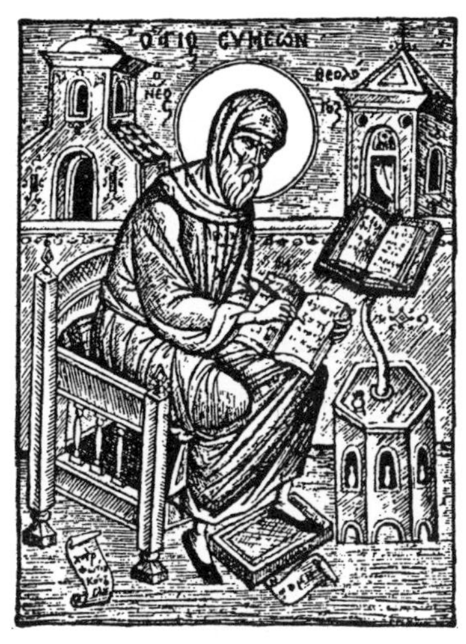

ST. SYMEON THE
NEW THEOLOGIAN

MONOGRAPHIC SUPPLEMENT SERIES
NUMBER VI

CONSTANTINE CAVARNOS

SMOKING AND THE ORTHODOX CHRISTIAN

Translated from the Greek by
Bishop Chrysostomos of Etna

CENTER FOR TRADITIONALIST
ORTHODOX STUDIES
Etna, California 96027
1992

18

*SMOKING AND THE ORTHODOX CHRISTIAN**

Smoking and the Orthodox Christian draws heavily from the *Handbook of Counsel* and *Spiritual Exercises* of St. Nicodemos the Hagiorite and from contemporary medical literature to argue that all should desist from smoking.

In texts taken from his two books, St. Nicodemos emphasizes that all clergymen should desist from smoking, because smoking is unbecoming to the high calling of the priesthood and episcopacy, and because the habit of smoking is very detrimental to the health of the body. Nicodemos also stresses that smoking is precluded for Christians in general, because it is a sinful habit, one that enslaves man and harms his body.

---

* Published in *The Patristic and Byzantine Review*, Vol. 13, Nos. 1, 2, 3, 1994, p. 142.

ΚΩΝΣΤΑΝΤΙΝΟΥ Π. ΚΑΒΑΡΝΟΥ
Καθηγητοῦ Πανεπιστημίου

ΤΟ ΚΑΠΝΙΣΜΑ
ΚΆΙ Ο ΟΡΘΟΔΟΞΟΣ ΧΡΙΣΤΙΑΝΟΣ

Περικοπαὶ ἀπὸ τὸ «Συμβουλευτικὸν Ἐγχειρίδιον» καὶ τὰ «Πνευματικὰ Γυμνάσματα» τοῦ **ΑΓΙΟΥ ΝΙΚΟΔΗΜΟΥ ΤΟΥ ΑΓΙΟΡΕΙΤΟΥ,** *καθὼς καὶ πολλαὶ Ἐρωτήσεις καὶ Ἀπαντήσεις διὰ τὸ κάπνισμα καὶ τὴν σχέσιν του πρὸς τὴν ὑγείαν, βάσει τῆς σημερινῆς Ἰατρικῆς Ἐπιστήμης, ὡς καὶ πρακτικαὶ συστάσεις διὰ τὴν ἀντιμετώπισιν τοῦ προβλήματος τοῦ παθητικοῦ (ἀκουσίου) καπνίσματος.*

ΝΕΑ, ΠΟΛΥ ΕΠΗΥΞΗΜΕΝΗ ΕΚΔΟΣΙΣ

ΕΚΔΟΣΕΙΣ «ΟΡΘΟΔΟΞΟΥ ΤΥΠΟΥ»
ΚΑΝΙΓΓΟΣ 10 — 106 77 ΑΘΗΝΑΙ 1988

Two chapters: (1) "Questions and Answers about Smoking," and (2) "Coping with the Problem of Passive Smoking," summarize what *medical authorities* now unhesitatingly and forcefully say about smoking.

Moral, religious, and medical arguments are joined to provide a compelling argument against smoking for all, not just for Orthodox clergy and laity.

ΚΩΝΣΤΑΝΤΙΝΟΥ ΚΑΒΑΡΝΟΥ
Καθηγητοῦ Πανεπιστημίου

ΟΔΟΙ ΚΑΙ ΤΡΟΠΟΙ ΠΡΟΣ ΤΗΝ ΑΓΙΟΤΗΤΑ

«Ἁγιασθήσεσθε καὶ ἅγιοι ἔσεσθε, ὅτι ἅγιός εἰμι ἐγὼ Κύριος ὁ Θεὸς ὑμῶν».

ΕΚΔΟΣΕΙΣ
"ΟΡΘΟΔΟΞΟΥ ΤΥΠΟΥ„

ΑΘΗΝΑΙ, 1980

KONSTANTINOS KAVARNOS

PYHITYKSEN TIE

PYHIEN ISIEN OPETUKSIA

SUOMENTANUT PETRI PIIROINEN

PATHS AND MEANS TO HOLINESS

by Constantine Cavarnos

Translated and Edited by

Bishop Chrysostomos of Oreoi

CENTER FOR TRADITIONALIST
ORTHODOX STUDIES

Etna, California 96027
1986

19

PATHS AND MEANS
*TO HOLINESS**

*C*onstantine Cavarnos' *Paths and Means to Holiness* has now had at least four lives. It was originally delivered in English as "The Ways of Sanctity," at the Orthodox Theological Seminary of Saint Tikhon of Zadonsk in South Canaan, Pennsylvania, on October 3, 1978, as part of the series "Called to Be Saints." It was published in the seminary's yearbook, *Tikhonaire*, in May of 1979. A Greek version appeared in serial form in Athens in *Orthodox Press* from August 31 to October 5, 1979. This Greek version was then published as a small book with prologue, epilogue, amplifications in the main text, indexes, and many hagiographical

---

* Published in *The Greek Orthodox Theological Review*, Vol. 32, No. 4, 1987, pp. 425-426.

illustrations in 1980. A second edition followed in 1985. Now we have a fourth appearance in a new translation by His Grace, Bishop Chrysostomos of Oreoi. This edition is based on the Greek text of the second, enlarged Athens edition of 1985. It reads exceptionally well, and the two appendices: "A Discourse on Monasticism," and "A Discourse for Those Living in the World" add to the attractiveness and usefulness of the volume.

It would not be amiss to say that Cavarnos' *Paths and Means to Holiness* has become something of a religious *classic*. Using Biblical and Patristic sources, the author demonstrates that the Orthodox Christian views the saint as one who has partaken of Divine grace, is inspired and guided by the Holy Spirit, is free from every vice, and is a possessor of every virtue: faith, hope, patience, humility, chastity, spiritual love, etc. Six categories of saints are enumerated: Apostles, Martyrs, Prophets, Hierarchs, Monastic saints, and the Righteous. Saint Peter Damascene has listed the first five; Saint Nicodemos the Hagiorite added the sixth.

Askesis, spiritual endeavor or training, is necessary for achieving holiness. It embraces bodily practices and mental practices. The physical practices include fasting, vigils, standing, prostrations, and silence. The spiritual practices involve repentance, concentration, meditation, inner attention, and prayer. More than anything else, prayer is noted as drawing Divine grace to man and uniting him with God.

Cavarnos concludes the main body of his work with this statement: "In a word, from this union is born the *theosis* of man, which is longed for by all, . . . and is the final end and purpose, God's foremost and highest goal" (p. 30).

Paths and Means to Holiness provides eloquent testimony to the Scriptural and Patristic basis of the Orthodox Christian spirituality and Greek Orthodox theology. It also provides highly readable, highly competent, and highly authoritative presentations of some of the most fundamental aspects of Greek Orthodox religiosity.

ΚΩΝΣΤΑΝΤΙΝΟΥ Π. ΚΑΒΑΡΝΟΥ
ΚΑΘΗΓΗΤΟΥ ΠΑΝΕΠΙΣΤΗΜΙΟΥ

Η ΜΕΛΛΟΥΣΑ ΖΩΗ ΚΑΤΑ ΤΗΝ ΟΡΘΟΔΟΞΟΝ ΔΙΔΑΣΚΑΛΙΑΝ

ΕΚΔΟΣΕΙΣ
"ΟΡΘΟΔΟΞΟΥ ΤΥΠΟΥ,,

ΑΘΗΝΑΙ 1984

KONSTANTINOS
KAVARNOS

ORTODOKSINEN OPETUS

Kuoleman-jälkeisestä elämästä

Suomentanut
Petri Piiroinen

THE FUTURE LIFE ACCORDING TO ORTHODOX TEACHING

by Constantine Cavarnos

translated by
Hieromonk Auxentios and
Archimandrite Chrysostomos

Foreword by
Archimandrite Chrysostomos

CENTER FOR TRADITIONALIST
ORTHODOX STUDIES
Etna, California 96027
1985

20

*THE FUTURE LIFE**

*T*he availability of *The Future Life According to Orthodox Teaching* in a magnificent English rendering by Fathers Auxentios and Chrysostomos of St. Gregory Palamas Monastery in Etna, California, is certainly a very welcome event. The seven chapters of this marvellous little book discuss "The Future Life According to Orthodox Teaching;" "Jesus Christ on the Soul;" "The Soul According to the Fathers of the Church;" "The Survival of the Soul after Death According to Holy Scripture;" "The Fathers of the Church on the Immortality of the Soul;" "The Immortality of the Soul in Orthodox Hymnography;" and "Holy Scripture on the Resurrection of the Dead and the Second Coming."

----

* Published in *St. Vladimir's Theological Quarterly*, Vol. 30, No. 2, 1986, pp. 178-179.

The committed Orthodox Christian could ask for no more clear, compact, and fully documented treatment of the subject, and the non-Orthodox will be impressed by the clarity of the exposition and cogency of the arguments made from Scriptural and Patristic sources.

In his Foreword, Archimandrite Chrysostomos acknowledges that "From the Patristic and Scriptural references which Cavarnos has collected with such assiduity, there flows forth that 'theology of facts' that so vibrantly enlivened the writings of the early Christian Fathers. If one rises above the merely scholarly and its limitations, he senses — as if with some hidden intuitive faculty — that what he is reading on the afterlife is not the result of frivolous speculation or personal presumption, but just what it is, a description rendered by those who saw, and then wrote about life after death" (p. 10).

Much has been added to this new English edition from Scriptural and Patristic sources that was not in the original Greek version published in 1984 by "Orthodox Press" of Athens. The translators have given us a splendid, if slightly different rendering from the original Greek version.

In *The Future Life According to Orthodox Teaching*, Dr. Cavarnos indicates that for the Orthodox Christian, death does not constitute annihilation: there is a continuation of the human soul apart from the body. This he makes abundantly clear. The Orthodox believe that the soul, even when separated from the body, continues to possess self-consciousness, to think with clarity, to possess feeling, to retain an integral memory.

However, it is also emphasized that the Church concerns herself with the whole person — physical and spiritual — and her teachings in this regard are embodied in Scripture, in the writings of the holy Fathers of the Church (especially the ascetics and mystics), in the lives of the saints, in church hymnody and iconography. The Orthodox Church does not believe in Purgatory. At the Final Judgment, bodies are reunited with souls. Those bodies will be spiritual, insusceptible of corruption and death.

This book should experience long and continuous use. It clearly demonstrates once again that in Constantine Cavarnos we have an indefatigable scholar and prolific writer, a committed Orthodox Christian teacher who will continue to illuminate us all about the Orthodox Church and provide valuable resource material for those who would seek to learn genuinely about this Church and its Tradition.

BIBLIOGRAPHICAL DATA
ON THE BOOKS REVIEWED

Sometimes several editions of a work are listed.
The first one in the list is the one that is
reviewed in this volume.

(1) *The Hellenic-Christian Philosophical Tradition*: Four Lectures delivered at Boston University. With an Introduction by Professor Stephen D. Salamone of Boston University. Belmont, Massachusetts: Institute for Byzantine and Modern Greek Studies, 1989. Pp. 137. (For brevity, henceforth the Institute will be listed as IBMGS.)

(2) *Modern Greek Thought*: Second printing. IBMGS, 1986. Pp. 115.

(3) *A Dialogue between Bergson, Aristotle, and Philologos*: A Comparative and Critical Study of Some Aspects of Henri Bergson's Theory of Knowledge and of Reality. Third, enlarged edition. IBMGS, 1988. Pp. 80.

(4) *Photian Studies*. Edited by George Papademetriou. Chapters by Panagiotes Chrestou, Stanley Harakas, George Bebis, Constantine Cavarnos, Emmanuel

Mikroyannakis, Metropolitan Emilianos Timiades, and George D. Gregory. Brookline, Massachusetts: Holy Cross Orthodox Press, 1989. Pp. 86.

(5) Dostoievsky's *Philosophy of Man.* Etna, California: Center for Traditionalist Orthodox Studies, 1987. Pp. 14. (For brevity, henceforth the Center will be listed as C.T.O.S.)

(6) *Synantéseis me ton Kóntoglou* ("Meetings with Kontoglou"). Athens, Ekdotikós Oíkos "Astér" of Al. & E. Papademetríou, 1985. Pp. 224.

Meetings with Kontoglou. First English-language edition. IBMGS, 1992 Pp. 214.

(7) *New Library, Volume I*: Reviews and discussions of over fifty books of Modern Greek, American, Russian and other writers pertaining to Philosophy — Ancient, Byzantine and Modern Greek —, Eastern Orthodox Christianity, Byzantine Art, and Hellenism. IBMGS, 1989. Pp. 176.

(8) *St. Cosmas Aitolos*: Great Missionary, Awakener, Illuminator, and holy Martyr of Greece. IBMGS, 1985. Pp. 118. Third, revised and considerably enlarged, edition. (First edition 1971.)

St. Cosmas d'Etolie: Hieromartyr Egal-aux-Apotres. 1714-1779. Par Constantin Cavarnos. Fête: 24 août. Lavardac: Monastère Orthodoxe Saint-Michel,

1991. Pp. 72. A French edition of the third English-language edition listed above, translated by Archimandrite Antoine Contamin, also known as Père Antoine de Lavardac, because of his association with the Monastery of Saint-Michel at Lavardac, France.

(9) *St. Nikephoros of Chios*: Outstanding Writer of Liturgical Poetry and Lives of Saints, Educator, Spiritual Striver, and Trainer of Martyrs. IBMGS, 1986. Pp. 124. Second edition. (First edition 1976.)

(10) *St. Nectarios of Aegina*: Metropolitan of Pentapolis, great Theologian, Philosopher, Moralist, Educator, Ascetic, Mystic, Miracle-Worker and Healer. IBMGS, 1988. Pp. 222. Second edition. (First edition 1981.)

(11) *St. Methodia of Kimolos*: Remarkable Ascetic, Teacher of Virtue, Counselor, Comforter and Healer (1863-1908). IBMGS, 1987. Pp. 123.

(12) *Sts. Raphael, Nicholas, and Irene*: Newly manifested Saints, who suffered Martyrdom by the Ottoman Turks in 1463 at the Monastery of the Nativity of the Theotokos near the village of Thermi on the Island of Lesvos. IBMGS, 1990. Pp. 200.

(13) *The Significance of the New Martyrs in the Life of the Orthodox Church*. Translated by Patrick G.

Barker. Monographic Supplement Series, Number IV. C.T.O.S ., 1992. Pp. 20.

The original, Greek text: *He Semasía ton Neomartyron eis ten Zoén tes Orthodóxou Ekklesías*, was published serially in the Athenian religious weekly *Orthodoxos Typos* ("Orthodox Press") from January 3 to February 14, 1992.

(14) *Orthodox Tradition and Modernism.* Translated by Patrick G. Barker. Monographic Supplement Series, Number V. C.T.O.S., 1992. Pp. 40.

The original, Greek text: *He Orthódoxos Parádosis kai ho Synchronismós.* Athens, Ekdoseis "Orthodoxou Typou," 1971. Pp. 55.

(15) *The Question of Union.* Translated by Patrick G. Barker. With a Preface by Photios Kontoglou and Foreword by Bishop Chrysostomos. C.T.O.S., 1992. Pp. 52.

The original, Greek text: *To Zétema tes Henóseos.* Preface and icons by Photios N. Kontoglou. Athens: Ekdoseis "Orthodoxou Typou," 1964. Pp. 32. Second edition, 1968, pp. 39.

(16) *Father Georges Florovsky on Ecumenism.* Monographic Supplement Series, Number VII. C.T.O.S., 1992. Pp. 15.

(17) *Nesteía kai Epistéme* ("Fasting and Science"). Athens: Ekdoseis "Orthodoxou Typou," 1988. Pp. 80.

English language edition: *Fasting and Science*. Translation of the first half of the original, Greek edition, by Bishop Chrysostomos and Hieromonk Auxentios. Monographic Supplement Series, Number III. C.T.O.S., 1988. Pp. 21.

(18) *Smoking and the Orthodox Christian*. Translated from the Greek by Bishop Chrysostomos of Etna. Monographic Supplement Series, Number VI. C.T.O.S., 1992. Pp. 22.

The original, Greek edition: *To Kápnisma kai ho Orthódoxos Christianós*. Athens: Ekdoseis "Orthodoxou Typou," 1988. Pp. 42. Reprinted 1994.

(19) *Paths and Means to Holiness*. Translated and edited with a Preface by Bishop Chrysostomos. C.T.O.S., 1985. Pp. 57.

The original, Greek edition: *Hodoí kai Trópoi Pros ten Hagióteta*. Athens: Ekdoseis "Orthodoxou Typou," 1980. Pp. 55. Second, enlarged edition, 1985. Pp. 71.

Finnish edition: *Pyhityksen Tie*. Translated by Petri Piiroinen. Joensuu, Finland: Ortokirja, 1988. Pp. 104.

(20) *The Future Life According to Orthodox Teaching*. Translated by Hieromonk Auxentios and Archimandrite Chrysostomos. Foreword by Archimandrite Chrysostomos. C.T.O.S., 1985. Pp. 88.

The original, Greek edition: *He Méllousa Zoé kata ten Orthódoxon Didaskalían*. Athens: Ekdoseis "Orthodoxou Typou," 1984. Pp. 79. Reprinted 1993.

Finnish edition: *Kuolemanjälkeisestä Elämästä*. Translated from the Greek edition by Petri Piiroinen, Joensuu: Ortokirja, 1990. Pp. 107.

INDEX OF PROPER NAMES

INDEX OF SUBJECTS

COMMENTS ON VOLUME I
(*AN EXPLORER OF REALMS OF ART, LIFE AND THOUGHT: A SURVEY OF THE WORKS OF CONSTANTINE CAVARNOS*)

In *An Explorer of Realms of Art, Life and Thought*, Professor John E. Rexine, Chairman of the Classics Department at Colgate University and also a Harvard graduate, briefly surveys 33 books written by Constantine Cavarnos between 1949 and 1985. Dr. Rexine is the author of several books (including *The Hellenic Spirit: Byzantine and Post-Byzantine*), many articles and more than one thousand book reviews. The reviews that make up this volume are culled from the pages of a dozen newspapers and journals, including *Athene, Balkan Studies, The Greek Orthodox Theological Review*, and *Saint Vladimir's Quarterly*.

Cavarnos' works are not difficult to categorize, so Dr. Rexine's reviews fit neatly into three parts. The first deals with 11 philosophical works, beginning with the first book, *A Dialogue between Bergson, Aristotle, and Philologos*, which won him the prestigious

Bowdoin Prize at Harvard in 1947. Other books are devoted to Plato's view of man, modern Greek philosophers, American philosophers, the English philosopher G.E. Moore, Byzantine thought, and the educational system of Benjamin of Lesvos.

Under the heading "Works on Orthodox Christian Art, Life, and Thought" are reviewed 14 books: on Byzantine art and music, Orthodox monasticism, Orthodox tradition and theology. Among these are two fascinating books on Mount Athos: *Anchored in God* (1959) and *The Holy Mountain* (1973).

The third part of Rexine's survey is devoted to Dr. Cavarnos' unique series *Modern Orthodox Saints*, among them Cosmas Aitolos (1714-1779), Macarios of Corinth (1731-1805), Arsenios of Paros (1800-1877) and the much beloved Nectarios of Aegina (1846-1920). These latter-day saints are rather remarkable men as Cavarnos' accounts of their lives, characters and messages demonstrate.

The reviews are supplemented by a short preface, a short introduction and a bibliography of Cavarnos' extensive work — selected articles and pamphlets as well as books. The collection of reviews adds up to an apparently comprehensive overview of Cavarnos' interests and total output.

I say "apparently" because many of the reviews are extremely brief — skeletal outlines at best in the cases of a number of books that surely merited more detailed discussion. Perhaps editors and space considerations can be blamed.

Professor Rexine is lavish in his praise; and Dr. Cavarnos was, and remains, an original and creative thinker.

— Steven Phillips, in the journal Greek Accent,
Vol. 6, No. 6, 1986.

This volume is devoted to the works of the distinguished Greek-American Orthodox philosopher-theologian Professor Constantine Cavarnos. In it, Professor John E. Rexine, a distinguished author in his own right, presents thirty-three reviews which he has written on as many of Cavarnos' books. In addition, he provides valuable biographical information on Dr. Cavarnos, and a complete list of his chief pamphlets, articles, and book reviews.

The book is carefully written and is a welcome addition to the Orthodox literature in America. Hopefully, it will be an impetus to all the readers to learn about classical and modern Greek thought, Byzantine culture and art, and especially the Orthodox

Christian experience reflected in the series *Modern Orthodox Saints*. This series, as well as his books on the Holy Mountain of Athos, on Byzantine art, and many other subjects, have been providing the American scholarly and religious public valuable knowledge on these realms.

We congratulate Dr. John E. Rexine for providing us with such a comprehensive volume. I recommend this excellent book to libraries to be used as a bibliographic reference, to scholars, and especially to Orthodox Christians in general, to learn about a prominent Greek-American Orthodox thinker, and lead them to the study of his highly recommended books.

— George C. Papademetriou,
Librarian and Professor of Theology,
Hellenic College / Holy Cross Greek
Orthodox School of Theology.

This beautifully bound and printed book is a rare one — and one long needed and desired by many. It is a book about one of the most outstanding and distinguished Greek-American scholars of the last three decades by an equally eminent scholar and friend of the former: a book by Professor John Rexine about Professor Constantine Cavarnos.

It is striking that both of these men were outstanding Harvard students, both *magna cum laude* at the baccalaureate level, both having earned their doctorates at Harvard, and both having distinguished themselves as Fulbright scholars. It is also worthy of note that both are trained in traditional, non-theological fields (Cavarnos in Philosophy and Rexine in the Classics), in which they have published widely, and yet have earned solid reputation as theologians.

This last fact, I might note parenthetically, has prompted the directors of the Center of Traditionalist Orthodox Studies, an eminent board of scholars, to elect them as recipients, in the spring of 1986, of the Center's Licentiate in Orthodox Theological Studies *honoris causa*, an honor bestowed on only one other person in the five-year history of the Center.

The book is essentially a compendium of the works of Dr. Cavarnos, containing reviews of his major publications (which include, to date, and astounding 33 books, countless articles, and numerous reviews). The importance of this book is that it fills a need: that of guiding the student or scholar in investigating the voluminous writings of this prolific man of letters.

I have myself experienced great frustration in trying to compile a collection of Cavarnos' writings, since, like those of Father Georges Florovsky, they are extraordinarily diverse and appear in literally a dozen different journals, in the case of articles, and cover a wide array of subjects, with regard to books.

As a solution to this problem of searching out materials, Dr. Rexine has brought together materials under three major sections: philosophical works; works on Orthodox Christian art, life and thought; and volumes on modern Orthodox saints. A very useful bibliography of Cavarnos' writings appears in the back of the book.

I heartily recommend this book to anyone who knows Cavarnos' work. It is an essential reference tool. As for those who do not know all of the writings of this scholar, the book is a proverbial "must."

As a tribute to a man who has excelled in letters, who has published important and celebrated volumes in both Greek and English, and who has stood firm in his dedication to the faith and culture of his Greek heritage, all Orthodox and all Greek-Americans should especially treasure this book.

— BISHOP CHRYSOSTOMOS,
of Etna, in *The Hellenic Chronicle*, 11-20-86

OTHER BOOKS BY CAVARNOS
PUBLISHED BY THE INSTITUTE FOR
BYZANTINE AND MODERN GREEK STUDIES
AFTER THOSE REVIEWED IN THIS VOLUME

THE SEVEN SAGES OF ANCIENT GREECE

The lives and teachings of the earliest Greek philosophers: Thales, Pittacos, Bias, Solon, Cleobulos, Myson, and Chilon. With English and Greek texts. 1996. Pp. 88.

PYTHAGORAS ON THE FINE ARTS AS THERAPY

A lecture delivered in 1993 at Wellesley College, sponsored by the History Department, the Classics Club, and the Hellenic Society of Wellesley College. Addressed to all who are interested in ancient Greek philosophy and culture in general, in the fine arts, in mental and physical health. 1994. Pp. 80.

SPIRITUAL BEAUTY

A discussion, in English and Greek, of Spiritual Beauty, with reference to philosophic, religious, and literary writings that date from Antiquity to the present. 1996. Pp. 62.

CULTURAL AND EDUCATIONAL CONTINUITY OF

GREECE FROM ANTIQUITY TO THE PRESENT

A discussion of a lecture delivered by the distinguished Argentine philosopher, philologist, and Hellenist Dr. Saúl A. Tovar. 1995. Pp. 75.

GREEK LANGUAGE AND CULTURE,

THEIR VITALITY AND IMPORTANCE TODAY

An eloquent, scholarly, and thought-provoking lecture by the late Harvard Professor of Classical Literature Cedric H. Whitman. Edited with Prefaces, Notes, Biographical Sketch, and an Appendix by Constantine Cavarnos. 1995. Pp. 56.

BYZANTINE CHURCHES OF THESSALONIKI

A discussion of the architecture and iconographic decoration of seven Byzantine churches of Thessaloniki—the second city of Greece as an administrative and cultural center—in a clear, simple, instructive, and fascinating way. 1995. Pp. 88.

ORTHODOX CHRISTIAN TERMINOLOGY

An illuminating lecture on the subject of developing a satisfactory, acceptable, standardized English-language terminology for Eastern Orthodox theology, hagiology, Church services, and the sacred arts, together with Greek-English and English-Greek glossaries. 1994. Pp. 80.

ECUMENISM EXAMINED

A concise analytical discussion of the contemporary Ecumenical Movement, with special reference to the Orthodox Church. 1996. Pp. 64.

THE CONCEPT OF CHRISTIAN LOVE

A lecture delivered at Columbia University, together with a Swedish version of it which was made in Sweden and was published in a religious journal of that country. 1996. Pp. 63.